BASEL

reinhardt

Viktor Börlin

BASEL

Unspektakuläre Ansichten – Unspectacular Views

Basel   Unspektakuläre Ansichten – Unspectacular Views

Alle Rechte vorbehalten – all rights reserved
© 2016 Friedrich Reinhardt Verlag, Basel
Bilder, Gestaltung und Text – Photography, design and text: Viktor Börlin
Layout: Stefan Escher
Druck und Bindung – Printing and binding: Druckerei Uhl GmbH & Co. KG
Quelle Karte auf Seite 125 – Source of map on page 125:
Geodaten Kanton Basel-Stadt, 14. Februar 2016

ISBN: 978-3-7245-2171-6

Vorwort

Braucht es ein weiteres Fotobuch über Basel? Wenn das Ziel ist, die Stadt Basel auf Postkartenansichten zu reduzieren, dann mit Sicherheit nicht. Jedoch sind es oft die weniger bekannten Orte und Perspektiven, die den Charakter einer Stadt beschreiben, treffender, als dies die üblichen Fotomotive können. Die Bilder im vorliegenden Buch sollen Ortskundige aber auch Personen, die Basel weniger gut kennen, zu einer anderen Art des Betrachtens anregen. Denn es sind gerade die wenig beachteten Winkel im städtischen Umfeld, die – gekoppelt an persönliche Erinnerungen – einen ganz besonderen Reiz entfalten. Die daraus resultierende Auseinandersetzung mit dem Alltäglichen, «Unspektakulären», möge der Betrachterin und dem Betrachter den Zugang zu einem anderen, sehr liebenswerten Basel eröffnen.

Formal zeichnen sich die grossen Bilder dieses Buches dadurch aus, dass das zentrale Objekt durch mindestens zwei vertikale Linien vom übrigen Bildinhalt separiert wird. Diese Begrenzungen können Häuserreihen, Baumstämme, Stangen oder Ähnliches sein. Dadurch wird die oft wenig beachtete Umgebung miteinbezogen. Jedem grossen Bild steht eine Detailaufnahme gegenüber.

Die Reihenfolge der Bilder folgt keiner systematischen Ordnung. Damit wird unterstrichen, dass mit dem Buch keine dokumentarische Aufarbeitung der Stadt Basel angestrebt wurde. Einige Quartiere sind untervertreten, andern wurden vielleicht zu viele Bilder gewidmet. Es wird auch bewusst auf erklärende Texte verzichtet. Vor Ihnen liegt ein reines Bilderbuch.

Die Aufnahmestandorte der grossen Bilder sind auf Seite 124 beschrieben und in der Karte auf Seite 125 eingetragen. Sie helfen dem Betrachter, die Bilder in der Realität (oder eher der Realität zum Zeitpunkt der Aufnahme) nachzuvollziehen. Alle Bilder sind an Orten aufgenommen worden, die frei zugänglich sind. Viel Spass bei den Spaziergängen mit oder ohne Kamera!

Viktor Börlin; Juli 2016

Foreword

Is there a need for another photo book on Basel? Certainly not if the aim is to reduce the city to postcard views. Often it is the lesser-known places and perspectives which portray the character of a town more authentically than can those usually photographed. The pictures in this book may open people who know the town, but also those just a bit familiar with it, to another way of observing. For it is exactly the less obvious corners in a city which – when coupled with personal memories – hold a special attraction. The resulting distinction from the typical, the "unspectacular", may offer the viewer access to another, especially charming Basel.

The larger pictures of this book are characterized formally by a separation of the central object from the remaining content of the image by at least two vertical lines. These borders can be rows of houses, tree trunks, poles or similar objects. Structuring the pictures in this way draws in the often overlooked surroundings. A detail is shown on the page opposite each large picture.

The sequence of the pictures follows no systematic order. This is to emphasize that this book in no way aspires to be a documentary-style reappraisal of Basel. Some quarters are underrepresented; others may have too many pictures. Intentionally there are no explanatory texts. This is a pure picture book.

The locations where the large photographs were taken are described on page 124 and depicted on the map on page 125. They should help the viewer experience the images as they exist in reality (or rather existed at the time of capture). All the photographs were taken at places that are freely accessible. May you find much enjoyment in walks through the city, with or without camera!

Viktor Börlin; July 2016

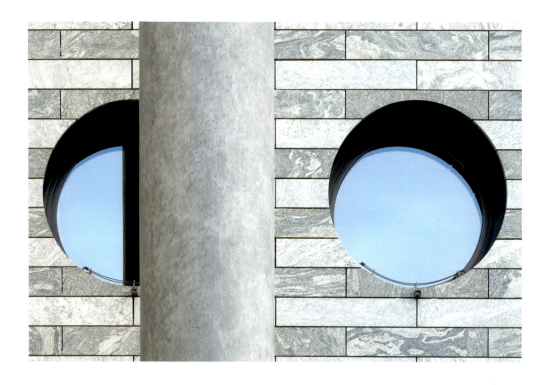

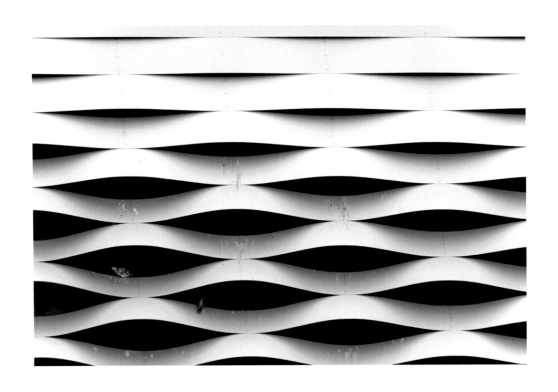

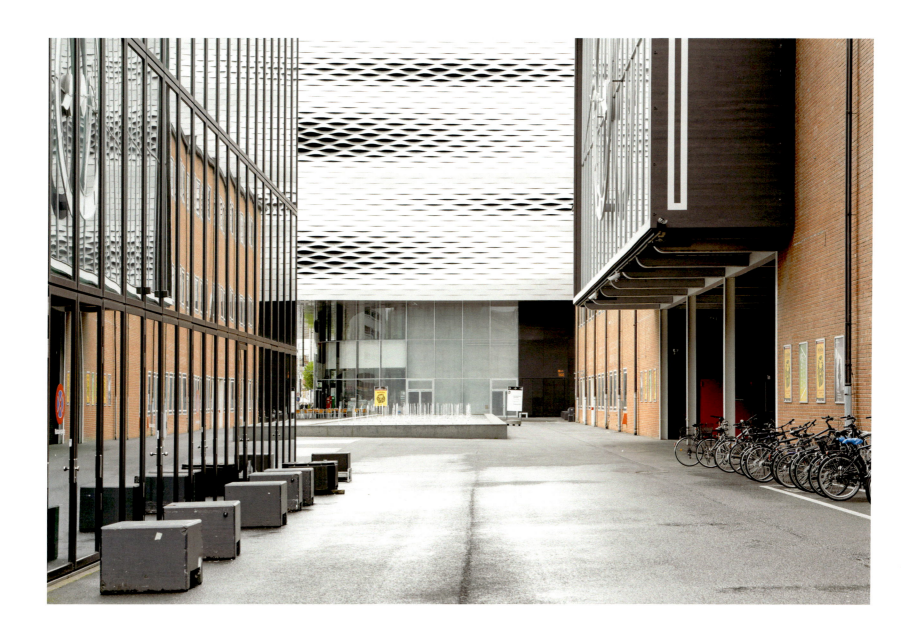

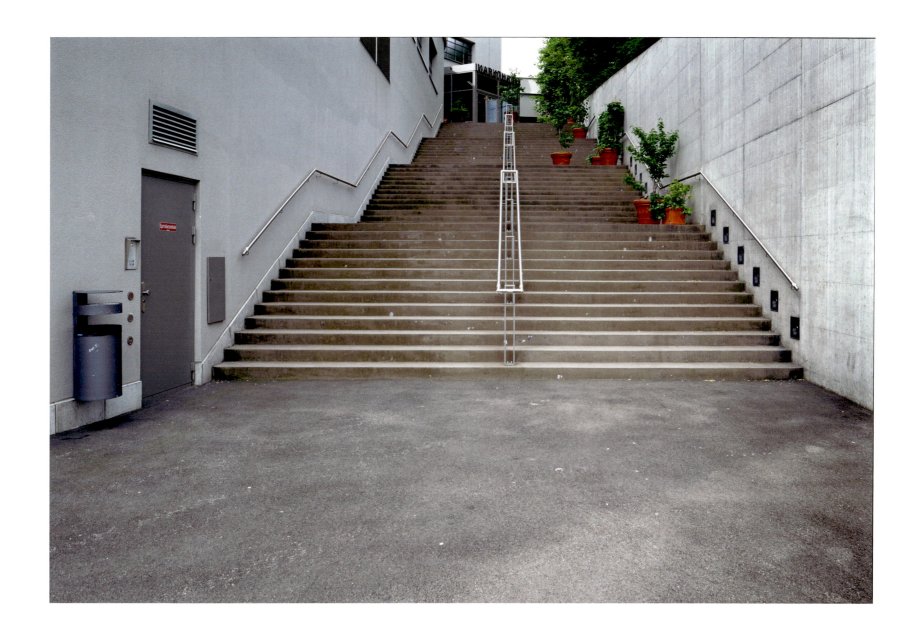

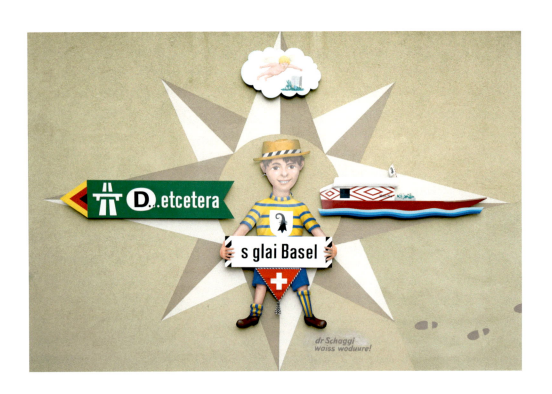

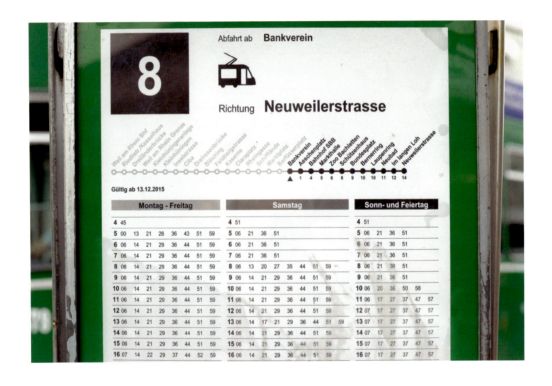

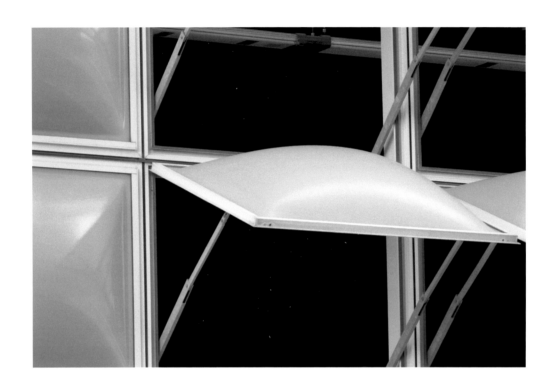

 ZUM VENEDIG

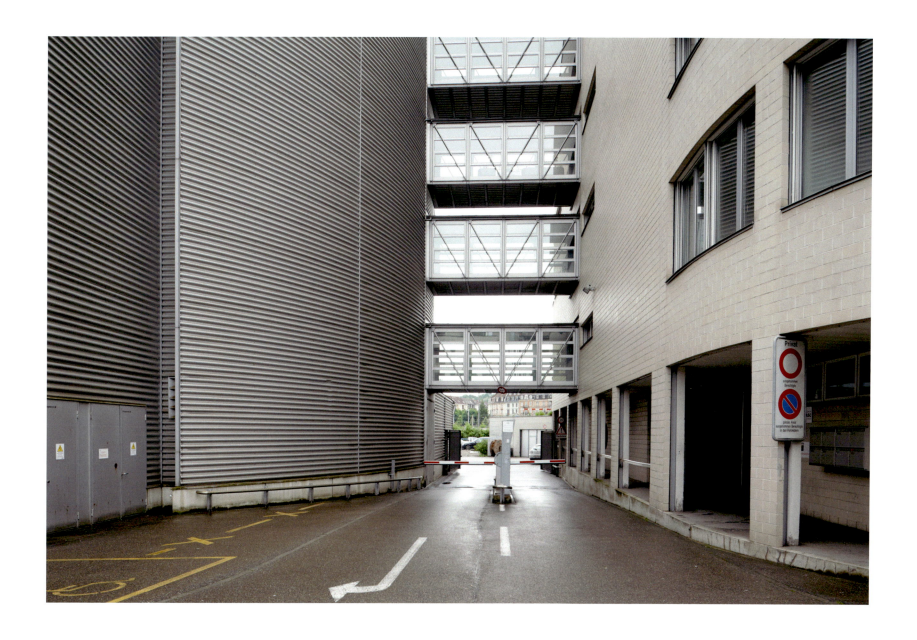

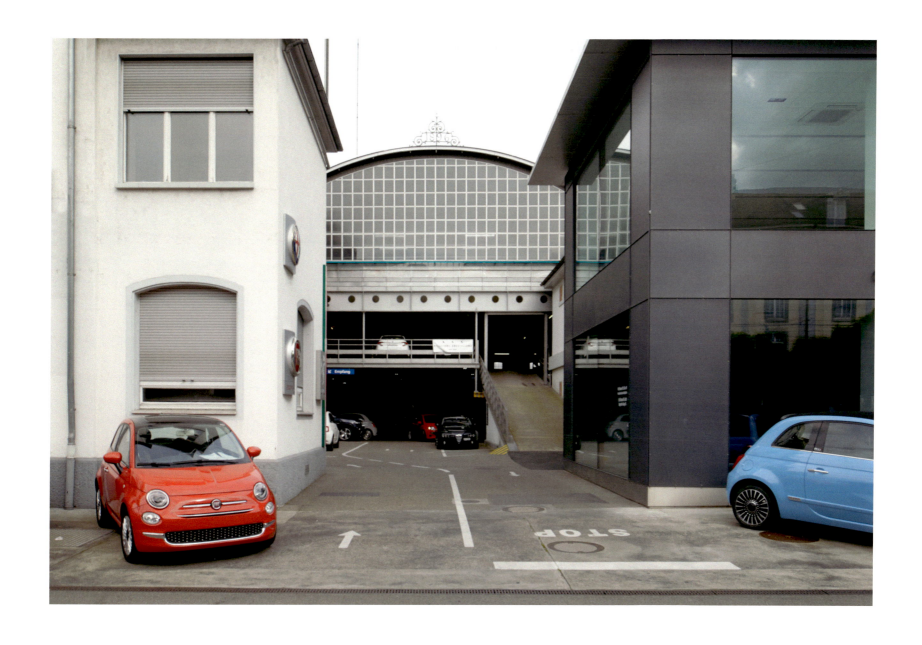

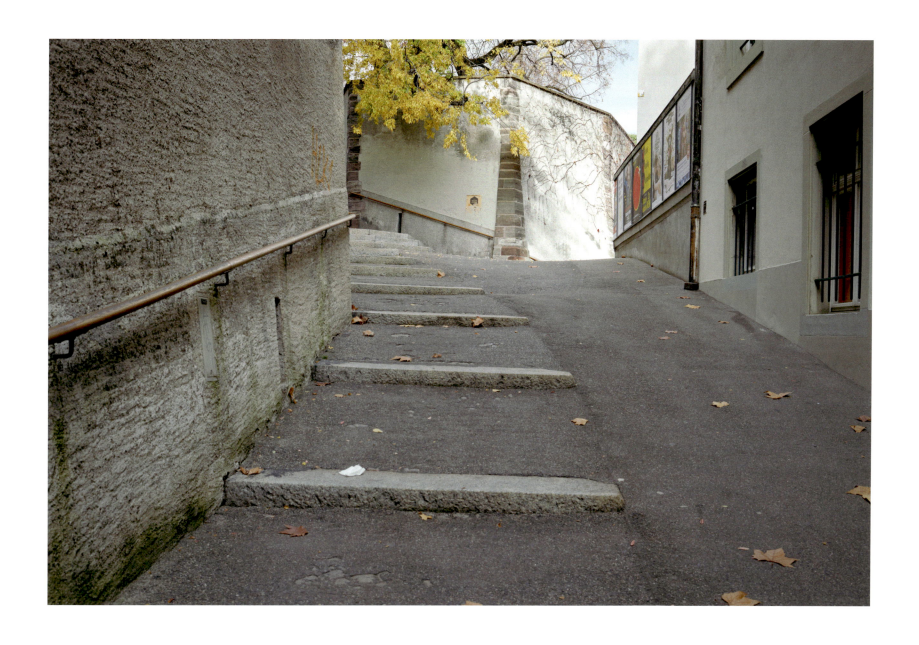

Aufnahmestandorte – Shooting locations

Nummern in ● = Seitenzahl Numbers in ● = Page Number

- **7** Aeschenplatz – BIZ-Gebäude (Building of Bank for International Settlements)
- **9** Basel SBB, Perron 11 und 12 (Basel Swiss Railway Station, Track 11 and 12)
- **11** Gerbergässlein
- **13** Messeplatz – Messe Basel, Halle 1 (Basel Fair, Hall 1)
- **15** Centralbahnplatz – Basel SBB (Basel Swiss Railway Station)
- **17** Gemsberg – Spalenberg
- **19** Steinentorberg – Treppe hinter Markthalle (Stairs behind Market Hall)
- **21** Küchengasse
- **23** Martinsgasse – Augustiner-Brunnen (Augustiner Fountain)
- **25** Nauenstrasse – Jacob Burckhardt-Haus
- **27** Tanzgässlein
- **29** Centralbahn-Passage
- **31** Centralbahnplatz – Strassburger Denkmal (Strasbourg Monument)
- **33** Grenzacherstrasse – Roche-Turm, Bau 1 (Roche-Tower, Building 1)
- **35** Sempacherstrasse
- **37** Spalenberg
- **39** Andreasplatz
- **41** Bauhinweglein – Wolfgottesacker, Friedhof (Wolfgottesacker, cemetery)
- **43** Münsterplatz – Andlauerhof
- **45** St. Alban-Kirchhof – St. Alban-Kirche (St. Alban Church)
- **47** Bäumleingasse
- **49** Maja Sacher-Platz – Museum für Gegenwartskunst (Museum of Contemporary Arts)
- **51** Südquaistrasse/Rheinhafen Hafenbecken 2 (Rhine Harbour Basin 2)
- **53** Im Wasenboden – Kehrichtverwertungsanlage (Refuse Incineration Plant)
- **55** Sempacherstrasse – Südpark
- **57** Theatergässlein/Steinenbachgässlein
- **59** Oetlingerstrasse – Musical Theater
- **61** Aeschenpassage
- **63** Südquaistrasse
- **65** Bruderholzrain
- **67** Gemsberg
- **69** Spitalstrasse – Universitätsspital, Klinikum 1 (University Hospital, Clinical Center 1)
- **71** Hafenstrasse
- **73** Rittergasse – Kunstmuseum, Neubau (Museum of Fine Arts, New Building)
- **75** Gerberpassage – Schmiedenhof
- **77** Markthallenbrücke – Markthalle (Market Hall)
- **79** Vogesenplatz
- **81** Glockengasse
- **83** St. Jakob-Park – Fussballstadion (Football/Soccer-Stadium)
- **85** Spalenvorstadt – Spalentor
- **87** Schlüsselberg
- **89** Parkweg
- **91** Mülhauserstrasse – Theobald Baerwart Schulhaus (Theodor Baerwart School)
- **93** Frankfurtstrasse/Mailandstrasse – Hindu Tempel (Hindu Temple)
- **95** Mailandstrasse
- **97** Totengässlein – Peterskirche
- **99** Beim Goldenen Löwen
- **101** Landhof
- **103** Wild Ma-Gässli
- **105** Grosspeterstrasse
- **107** Stapfelberg
- **109** Ziegelstrasse
- **111** Viaduktstrasse/Steinentorberg – Elsässertor
- **113** Margarethenstrasse
- **115** Malzgasse
- **117** Nadelberg/Spalenberg
- **119** Lohnhofgässlein
- **121** Schafgässlein/Rheingasse
- **123** Sperrstrasse/Riehenring

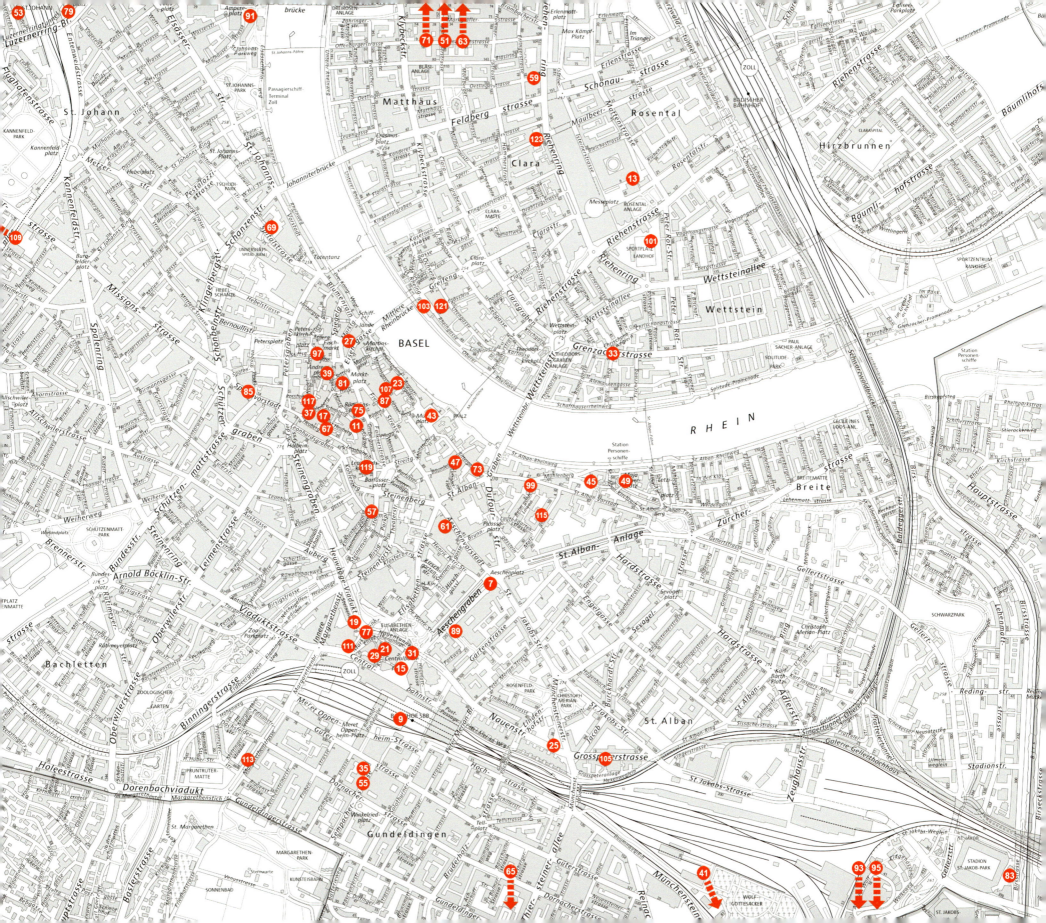

Fotograf

Viktor Börlin studierte Medizin an der Universität Basel. Den grössten Teil seiner beruflichen Karriere arbeitete er in den Forschungs- und Entwicklungsabteilungen bei Sandoz, Novartis und Hoffmann-La Roche. Er hatte während dieser Zeit Gelegenheit, in den USA und Japan zu leben. Diese Auslandsaufenthalte waren eine enorme Bereicherung für sein Leben und führten auch dazu, dass er die einzigartige Basler Atmosphäre vermehrt zu schätzen begann.
Als Fotograf war Viktor Börlin zu Beginn Autodidakt und lernte viel bei seiner Arbeit in der eigenen Dunkelkammer. Nach der Umstellung von Analog- auf Digitalfotografie war er enttäuscht von der Qualität seiner Bilder und besuchte deswegen mehrere Seminarien zu Bildbearbeitung und Fine Art Printing. Seit seiner Pensionierung geniesst es der passionierte Hobbyfotograf, seinen fotografischen Projekten mehr Zeit und Energie widmen zu können.

Erwerb von Buch und Fine Art Prints – www.viktorboerlin.com

Photographer

Viktor Börlin graduated with an MD degree from Basel University Medical School. He spent most of his professional career in Research and Development Departments of Sandoz, Novartis and Roche. During this time, he had the opportunity to live in the USA and Japan. These stays abroad were an enormous personal enrichment and also helped increase his appreciation of the unique atmosphere of Basel.
As a photographer, Viktor Börlin initially was self-taught and learned a lot from work in his own darkroom. After the switch from analog to digital photography he was so disappointed in his results that he decided to attend several workshops on digital image processing and fine art printing. Now that he is retired from his profession, the avid amateur photographer enjoys being able to devote more time and energy to his photographic projects.

For purchase of book and fine art prints – www.viktorboerlin.com

Danke

«Basel – Unspektakuläre Ansichten» wäre ohne die Unterstützung von Freunden, Bekannten und meiner Familie gar nicht oder in einer andern Form erschienen. Einen wichtigen Beitrag haben auch meine Lehrer im Fach Fotografie für das vorliegende Buch geleistet. Sie haben versucht, mir Bildgestaltung und -bearbeitung beizubringen. Folgenden Leuten bin ich für ihre Beiträge sehr dankbar:

Thank you

Without support from friends, acquaintances and my family, «Basel – Unspectacular Views» never would have been published or would have appeared in a different form. My photography teachers also have contributed significantly to this book. They tried to teach me the essentials of image composition and editing. I sincerely thank the following persons for their contributions:

Caroline Barthe, Christoph Bauer, Aurelio Börlin, Katherina Börlin, Raphael Börlin, Roberto Casavecchia, Ralph Dinkel, Stephanie Ehret, Stefan Escher, Ferit Kuyas, Michael Martin, Susan Mellen, Felix Rudolf von Rohr, Monika Wertheimer und Markus Zuber.